SOP for Conducting Sea Otter Aerial Surveys — Version 1.2

Southwest Alaska Inventory and Monitoring Network

Natural Resource Report NPS/SWAN/NRR—2011/393

James L. Bodkin[1]

[1]U.S. Geological Survey
Alaska Science Center,
4210 University Dr
Anchorage, AK 99508

May 2011

U.S. Department of the Interior
National Park Service
Natural Resource Program Center
Fort Collins, Colorado

The National Park Service, Natural Resource Program Center publishes a range of reports that address natural resource topics of interest and applicability to a broad audience in the National Park Service and others in natural resource management, including scientists, conservation and environmental constituencies, and the public.

The Natural Resource Report Series is used to disseminate high-priority, current natural resource management information with managerial application. The series targets a general, diverse audience, and may contain NPS policy considerations or address sensitive issues of management applicability.

All manuscripts in the series receive the appropriate level of peer review to ensure that the information is scientifically credible, technically accurate, appropriately written for the intended audience, and designed and published in a professional manner. This report received formal peer review by subject-matter experts who were not directly involved in the collection, analysis, or reporting of the data, and whose background and expertise put them on par technically and scientifically with the authors of the information.

Views, statements, findings, conclusions, recommendations, and data in this report are those of the author(s) and do not necessarily reflect views and policies of the National Park Service, U.S. Department of the Interior. Mention of trade names or commercial products does not constitute endorsement or recommendation for use by the National Park Service.

This report is available from the Southwest Alaska Inventory & Monitoring Network website (http://science.nature.nps.gov/im/units/swan/) and the Natural Resource Publications Management website (http://www.nature.nps.gov/publications/nrpm/).

Please cite this publication as:

Bodkin, J. L. 2011. SOP for conducting sea otter aerial surveys - Version 1.2: Southwest Alaska Inventory and Monitoring Network. Natural Resource Report NPS/SWAN/NRR—2011/393. National Park Service, Fort Collins, Colorado.

NPS 953/107692, May 2011

Revision History Log

All edits and amendments made to this document since its inception should be recorded in the table below. Users of this protocol should promptly notify the project leader of the marine nearshore monitoring program of recommended edits or changes. The project leader will review and incorporate suggested changes as necessary, record these changes in the revision history log, and modify the date and version number on the title page of this document to reflect these changes.

Revision History Log:

Previous Version #	Revision Date	Author	Changes Made	Reason for Change	New Version #
Version 1	10/15/2007	Kloecker	Add revision table, header / footer		No new version
Version 1	08/12/2010	Coletti	Formatting; updating to reflect SWAN	To meet NRR standards, remove NGEM references	1.1
Version 1	1/16/2011	Bodkin	Edits	Final edit	1.2
Add rows as needed for each change or set of changes associated with each version.					

Contents

Contents (continued)

Figures

Tables

Appendices

1 Background and Objectives

1.1 Introduction

The purpose of this SOP is to provide rational for, and describe the sampling design and methods used to estimate the abundance and distribution of sea otter populations within the SWAN parks. These data will be used to detect changes in the density and distribution of this species over time.

The sea otter was selected as a mammalian representative of the nearshore trophic web for several reasons. First, as a top level predator and consumer of nearshore benthic invertebrates, food limitation is generally considered an important factor in regulating sea otter population size (Kenyon 1969, Riedman and Estes 1990, Bodkin 2003). Because of a high daily caloric requirement and an almost exclusive reliance on nearshore invertebrates as prey, the abundance of sea otters likely reflects the abundance and productivity of the nearshore ecosystem. Therefore, monitoring sea otter populations, in conjunction with measures of benthic invertebrate and algal communities, will allow inference to functional relations between producers and consumers in the nearshore community.

Secondly, sea otters are widely recognized for the role they play in structuring nearshore marine ecosystems (Estes and Bodkin 2002). Probably the best example of the role of sea otters as a keystone species in structuring marine communities comes from contrasting locations when sea otters are present in large numbers or absent, a consequence of the Pacific maritime fur trade that ended about 1900. At locations where sea otters were abundant, few sea urchins and well-developed kelp forests dominated the system, whereas abundant sea urchins had destroyed the kelp forests where sea otters were absent (Estes and Palmissano 1974). The explanation for this pattern is a direct result of what has since come to be known as a "trophic cascade". That is, sea urchin populations are regulated by sea otter predation, in turn allowing the kelp forest to flourish in the absence of significant herbivory. When otters were removed, sea urchins increased to such levels that deforestation occurred. Similar patterns between areas with and without sea otters have since been documented in southeast Alaska, British Columbia, Washington, and California (Estes and Duggins 1995). Similar trophic-cascades resulting from the effects of apex predators are now known for many systems (Power et al. 1996)

Numerous indirect effects of the sea otter-urchin-kelp trophic cascade are known or suspected. Most of these relate to the role of kelp as habitat and a source of production for other species of consumers in nearshore food webs. The kelps (order *Laminariales*) and other species of macroalgae are extremely productive, in large measure because none of the essential ingredients for photosynthesis (light, water, CO_2, and nutrients) are limiting in shallow coastal waters at high latitudes. Thus, systems with and without sea otters (and thus with and without well-developed kelp forests) vary substantially in total productivity with total production estimated to be 3-4 times greater where sea otters were present (Simenstead et al 1978).

Other indirect effects on higher trophic level consumers result from increased production, altered habitat, or competition with otters for common food resources. Examples include positive relations between sea otters and bald eagle (*Haliaetus leucocephalus*) and harbor seal (*Phoca vitulina*) densities, as well as negative relations with benthic feeding sea ducks which feed mainly on sea urchins, mollusks, and other benthic invertebrates, which occur at higher densities where otters are rare or absent than where sea otters are abundant.

Thirdly, sea otters are a species that suffered both extensive acute mortality, as well as long-term exposure mediated effects from the *Exxon Valdez* oil spill. More than a decade after the spill, sea otters remained exposed to lingering oil in the nearshore environments of western Prince William Sound, and have demonstrated delayed recovery. Because the burrowing infauna, primarily clams, that dominate the diet of sea otters in most soft sediment habitats in Alaska (Dean et al. 2002), require excavation, and co-occur where lingering oil persisted, sea otters residing in heavily oiled habitat exhibited significantly higher levels of the cytochrome P450 1A biomarker, than did otters living outside the spill zone (Bodkin et al 2002). Consequences of chronic exposure include elevated mortality rates, compared to pre-spill levels (Monson et al. 2000), and a population in western Prince William Sound that had failed to recover for more than 13 years following the spill (Bodkin et al. 2002).

And lastly, standardized, detection adjusted, and cost effective surveys of sea otter abundance have been developed, tested (Bodkin and Udevitz 1999) and implemented, throughout the Gulf of Alaska area, and when coupled with earlier surveys, offer an historic perspective of abundance for an important member of the nearshore fauna that may not be available for any other species.

1.2 Rationale for obtaining sea otter abundance data

Sea otters (*Enhydra lutris*) are a common, conspicuous, and important component of the nearshore trophic food web throughout the North Pacific. They occupy all types of nearshore habitats from sheltered bays, estuaries, and fjords to exposed rocky coastlines (Kenyon 1969), but are constrained by their diving ability to habitats shallower than 100 m depth (Bodkin et al. 2004) and a near exclusive dietary reliance on benthic invertebrate prey (Riedman and Estes 1991). As a consequence of their nearshore distribution and relatively small home ranges, a rich literature exists on the biology, behavior, and ecology of the species. The sea otter provides one of the best documented examples of top-down forcing effects on the structure and function of nearshore marine ecosystems in the North Pacific Ocean (Kenyon 1969, VanBlaricom and Estes 1988, Riedman and Estes 1990, Estes and Duggins 1995) and are widely regarded as a "keystone" species in coastal marine ecosystems (Power et al. 1996). They cause well described top-down cascading effects on community structure by altering abundance of prey (e.g. sea urchins) which can in turn alter abundance of lower trophic levels (e.g. kelps). Sea otters generally have smaller home ranges than other marine mammals; eat large amounts of food; are susceptible to contaminants such as those related to oil spills; and have broad appeal to the public. Recent declines in sea otters have been observed in the Aleutian Islands. As a result, the Western Alaska stock of sea otters, which occurs from Cook Inlet to the Western Aleutian Islands and includes KATM as well as Aniakchak National Monument and Preserve (ANIA), was federally listed on September 2005 as threatened under the Endangered Species Act (USFWS 70 FR 46366, 2005).

For the reasons outlined above, several metrics related to sea otters are incorporated under this vital sign. They include: aerial surveys to estimate population abundance, carcass collections to evaluate the age structure of the dying population, and observations of sea otter foraging. Because sea otters occur over a much larger area in than nearshore than sampled under the marine bird and mammal surveys and detection from skiffs is less than 1.0, aerial surveys designed specifically to provide accurate and precise estimates of sea otter abundance (Bodkin and
Udevitz 1999) are incorporated into the SWAN nearshore monitoring program.

1.3 Measurable Objective

Conducting sea otter aerial surveys to estimate long-term trends in sea otter abundance in KATM and KEFJ will allow us to answer the following questions:

- What is the density of sea otters in waters adjacent to the Parks?
- How is abundance of sea otters changing annually?
- Where do sea otters occur in waters adjacent to the Parks?

2 Sampling Design

2.1 Rationale for Selecting this Sampling Design over Others

Selection of a park unit as the sample area for sea otter populations was based on two factors, the mean home range and movements of the species, and the need for an area large enough to provide adequate sample sizes, in terms of intensive search units (ISU's) to provide population estimates with adequate precision (se < 0.20). Effective population monitoring requires the assumption that movements of individuals across survey boundaries are not responsible for changes in estimates over time. The validity of this assumption becomes less of a concern as the area of the survey unit increases relative to movements, or home ranges of individuals. Because the annual home ranges of sea otters in Alaska are on the order of 10's of km^2 (USGS Alaska Science Center, unpublished data) it is likely that movements of individuals into the survey area will approximate movement out of the survey area. Using the aerial survey method described by Bodkin and Udevitz (1999) requires a large enough sampling area to allow for the acquisition of a sample of 25-40 intensive search units. Intensive search units are searches of portions of a transect that are used to adjust counts for animals that are not detected while surveying transects. Prior surveys of sea otter abundance in western Prince William Sound demonstrate a sample area suitable for acquiring the necessary sample of ISU's to achieve the desired precision (% se < 0.20).

2.2 Overview of Survey Design

The survey design consists of 2 components: (1) strip transect counts and (2) intensive search units.

1. Strip Transect Counts

Sea otters are sampled within two habitat strata based on the anticipated density of otters (high or low) within those habitats. High and low density strata are distinguished by distance from shore and depth contour (Bodkin and Udevitz 1999, Appendix B). The high density stratum extends from shore to 400 m seaward or to the 40 m depth contour, whichever is greater. The low density stratum extends from the high density line to a line 2 km offshore or to the 100 m depth contour, whichever is greater. Bays and inlets less than 6 km wide are sampled entirely as high density, regardless of depth. Transects are spaced systematically from a random start point within each stratum, and are oriented in a direction predominately perpendicular to the shore. Survey effort is allocated proportional to expected otter abundance in the respective strata.

Transects with a 400-m strip width on one side of a fixed-wing aircraft are surveyed by a single observer. Transects are flown at an airspeed of 60 mph (26.8 m/s) and an altitude of 300 feet (91.5 m). The observer searches forward as far as conditions allow and out 400 m, indicated by marks on the aircraft struts, and records otter group size and location on a transect map. A group is defined as 1 or more otters spaced less than 3 otter lengths apart. Any group greater than 20 otters is circled until a complete count is made. A camera should be used to photograph any groups too large and concentrated to count accurately. The number of pups in a group is noted behind a slash (e.g. 6/4 = 6 adults and 4 pups). Observation conditions are noted for each transect and the pilot does not assist in sighting sea otters.

Each strip or block of water to be sampled will have two possible flight paths, an A side and a B side (see Figure 1 and 2). The observer chooses a side from which to survey depending on direction of glare so the same block of water will be sampled. Because this method involves choosing one of 2 sets of waypoints per block (a start and end coordinate for the A side or a start and end coordinate for the B side), the observer will select either an A card or a B card for each region to load into the GPS.

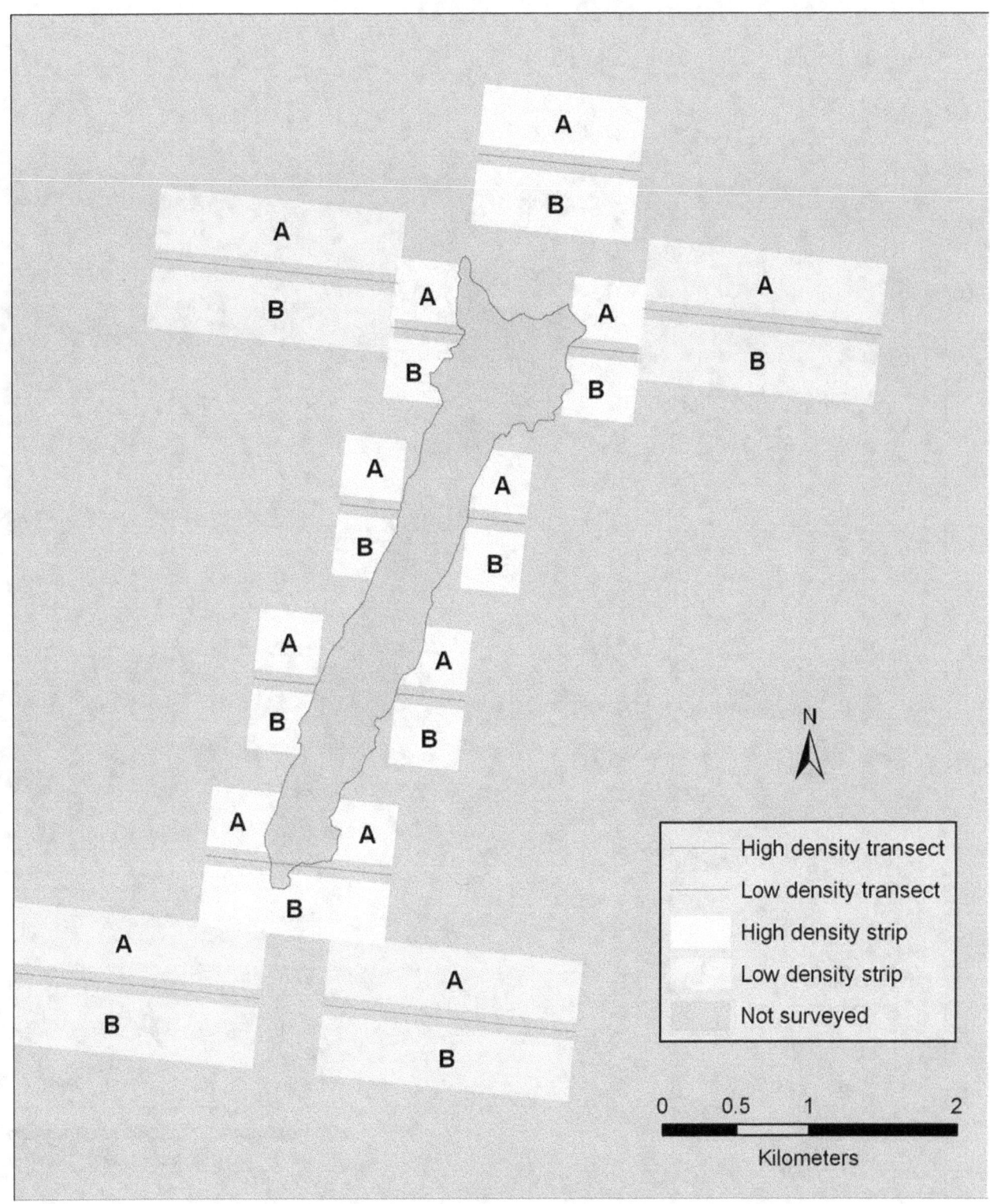

Figure 1. Diagram showing flight paths used for strip transect counts, an A side and a B side

Legend:
- High density transect
- Low density transect
- High density strip
- Low density strip
- Not surveyed

N

0   0.5   1   2
Kilometers

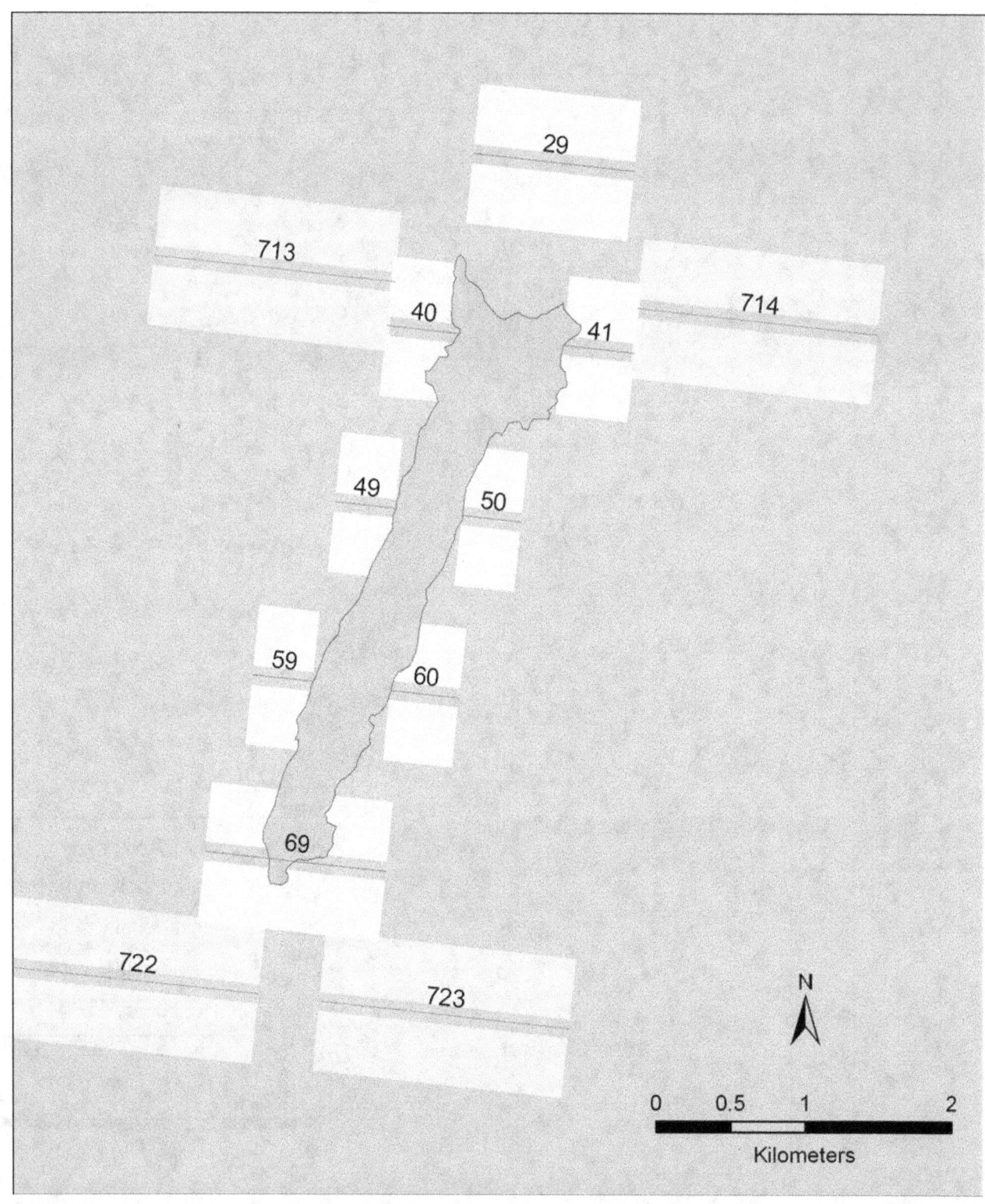

Figure 2. Survey map with transect numbers used to record strip transect counts. The blue lines are low density and the red lines are high density transects.

2. Intensive Search Units

Intensive search units (ISU's) are flown at intervals dependent on sampling intensity*, throughout the survey period. An ISU is initiated by the sighting of a group and is followed by 5 concentric circles flown within the 400 m strip perpendicular to the group which initiated the ISU. The pilot uses a stopwatch to time the minimum 1 minute spacing between consecutive ISU's and guide the circumference of each circle. With a circle circumference of 1,256 m and airspeed of 65 mph (29 m/sec), it takes 43 seconds to complete a circle (i.e. 11 seconds/quarter turn). With 5 circles, each ISU takes about 3.6 minutes to complete. ISU circle locations are drawn on the transect map and group size and activity is recorded on a separate form for each ISU. For each group, record number observed on the strip count and number observed during the circle counts. Otters that swim into an ISU post factum are not included and groups greater than 20 otters cannot initiate an ISU.

Behavior is defined as "whatever the otter was doing before the plane got there" and recorded for each group as either diving (d) or non-diving (n). Diving otters include any individuals that swim below the surface and out of view, whether traveling or foraging. If any individual(s) in a group are diving, the whole group is classified as diving. Non-diving otters are animals seen resting, interacting, swimming (but not diving), or hauled-out on land or ice.

* The targeted number of ISU's per hour should be adjusted according to sea otter density. For example, say we have an area that is estimated to take 25 hours to survey and the goal is to have each observer fly 40 "usable" ISU's; an ISU must have more than one group to be considered usable. Because previous data show that only 40 to 55% of the ISU's end up being usable, surveyors should average at least 4 ISU's per hour. Considering the fact that one does not always get 4 opportunities per hour, especially at lower sea otter densities, this actually means taking something like the first 6 opportunities per hour.

However, two circumstances may justify deviation from the 6 ISU's per hour plan:

> 1) if the survey is not progressing rapidly enough because flying ISU's is too time intensive, *reduce* the minimum number of ISU's per hour slightly

> 2) if a running tally begins to show that, on average, less than 4 ISU's per hour are being flown, *increase* the targeted minimum number of ISU's per hour accordingly.

The bottom line is this: the observer needs to obtain a preset number of ISU's for adequate statistical power in calculation of the correction factor. To arrive at this goal in an unbiased manner, observers must pace themselves so ISU's are evenly distributed throughout the survey area.

2.3 Choosing Sampling Units
See SWAN Nearshore Protocol (Dean and Bodkin 2010??)

2.4 Recommended Frequency and Timing of Sampling
See SWAN Nearshore Protocol (Dean and Bodkin 2010??)

2.5 Level of Change that can be Detected

Surveys of sea otter abundance have been conducted within Prince William Sound over the past 12 years (Bodkin et al, 2002, Table 1 below). We used the mean abundance data to estimate the number of additional surveys required to detect various levels of change (ranging from 20 to 70%) with 80% power (alpha 0.05) and to evaluate the effect of various sampling frequencies on the number of years of sampling required to detect a 50% change in abundance with 80% power. We estimated the number of additional samples required to detect various levels of change using a two-tailed t-test, with unequal sample sizes. Methods used are described in Cohen (1988). Specifically, we examined sample size requirements in a test of null hypothesis that the mean abundance of sea otters in outgoing years would not differ from the mean abundance observed over the previous 12 years (see Table 1 in which 11 surveys were performed).

Table 1. Surveys of sea otter abundance conducted within Prince William Sound for the past 12 years (J.L. Bodkin, unpublished data).

	Western PWS		
Date	Population size	Std. Error	Propor. SE
Aug-93	2,054	698	0.34
Aug-94	2,228	356	0.16
Jul-95	2,185	225	0.10
Jul-96	2,180	218	0.10
Jul-97	2,341	202	0.09
Jul-98	3,119	494	0.16
Jul-99	2,475	381	0.15
Jul-00	2,658	294	0.11
Jul-01	.	.	.
Jul-02	1,840	334	0.18
Jul-03	2,631	540	0.21
Jul-04	2,704	315	0.12

The number of additional samples required to detect various levels of change ranged from 1 (to detect a 70% change) to 10 (to detect a 20% change) (Fig. 3). An additional 2 surveys were required to detect between a 40 and 60% change in sea otter abundance. We used these results to predict the effect various sampling frequencies on our ability to detect a 50% change in sea otter abundance. Yearly surveys could detect a 50% change in two years while sampling every four years would require 5 to 8 years before the change could be detected (Fig.4). In the latter case, the range in years is dependent on when the change occurred relative to the initial year of sampling.

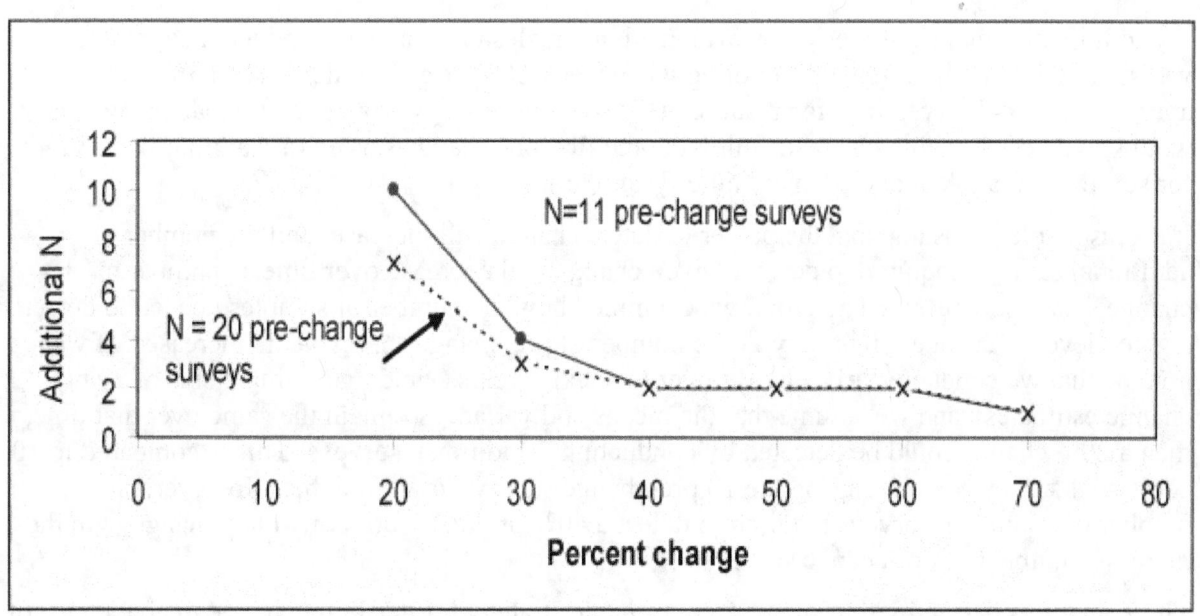

Figure 3. Number of additional samples required to detect a given change in sea otter abundance in Western Prince William Sound with 80% power.

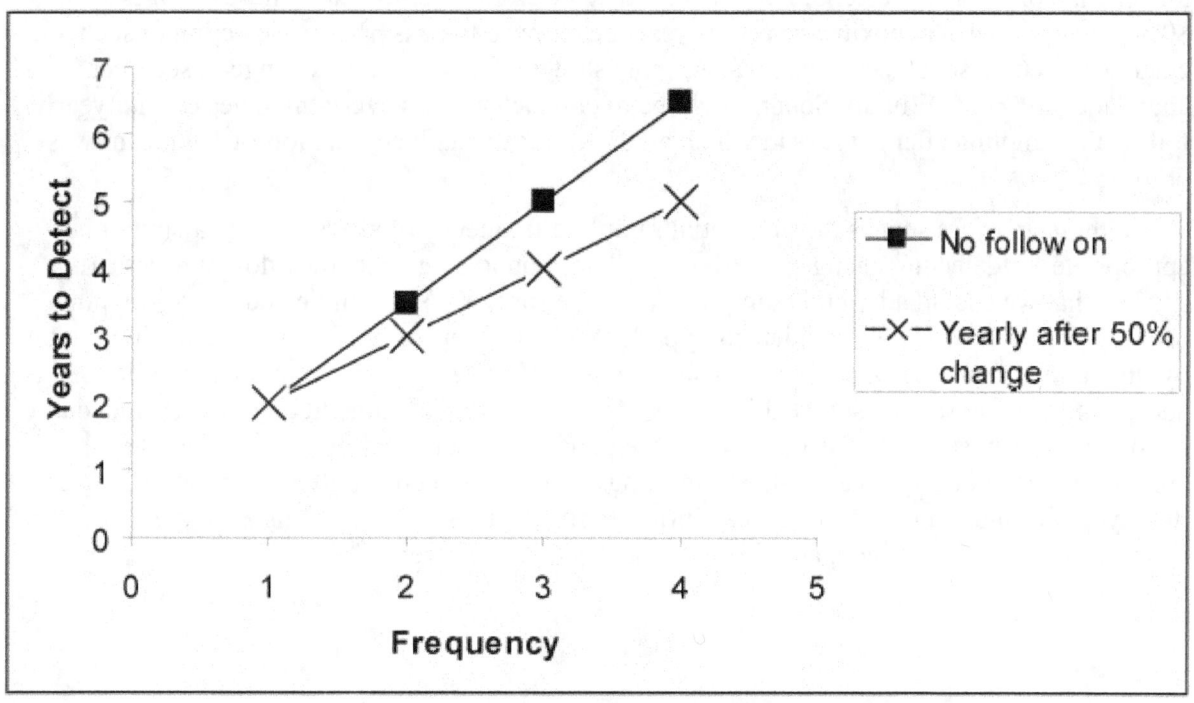

Figure 4. Additional years of sampling required to detect a 50% change in sea otter abundance in Western Prince William Sound with 80% power given different sampling frequencies

An additional sampling strategy was evaluated in which sampling was conducted every 2 to 4 years, but with yearly follow up sampling whenever a 50% or greater decrease in mean abundance was observed in a given survey (Fig.4). This strategy would ensure that any change would be detected within one year following the first pre-change survey (a maximum of 3 years for surveys initially conducted every other year, etc.).

It is reasonable to assume that the power to detect change will increase, and the number of additional samples required to detect a given change will decrease over time as number of pre-change surveys increases. Therefore, we examined how the number of samples needed to detect a given level of change might vary as the number of pre-change survey years increased. If we assume that we conduct yearly surveys over the next 9 years (yielding a sample size of 20 pre-change estimates), and we assume that the means and variances remain the same over that time, then a 20% change could be detected by conducting 7 additional surveys. This is compared to 10 additional surveys required using the 10 pre-change surveys now available. However, the number of additional surveys required to detect a 40% or greater effect will not change with the increased number of pre-change surveys.

These analyses can be used to suggest a reasonable strategy for detecting change in abundance of sea otters in Prince William Sound over time. But first, some judgments are required regarding the level of change that is of concern, the desired power to detect such a change, and how many years prior to detection is acceptable. For the purposes of planning, we have made the judgments that change of 50% or greater are of concern, that we would like to detect these changes with 80% power, and that a maximum of four years be allowed to pass prior to detection of such a change. Given these requirements, a reasonable strategy for detecting a change in sea otter abundance in Prince William Sound might be to conduct surveys every three years, with yearly follow up sampling after surveys in which a 50% change (relative to the long-term mean) was observed.

While these analyses suggest that an initial sampling frequency of every three years night be appropriate for detecting changes in Prince William Sound over time, they do not necessarily suggest that we should adopt this sampling schedule for SWAN. As indicated previously, the primary concerns of SWAN are detecting park - wide differences over time, or detecting region by time interactions. The analyses for a single region (Prince William Sound) can not be used to address power and sample size requirements for the broader questions. It is our recommendation to conduct yearly surveys of sea otters in all regions for 5 years, and then to conduct the appropriate power analyses and adjust sampling frequencies accordingly. Sampling once every three years would require some 15 years prior to making reasoned decisions as to the appropriateness of the design, and this is too long in our judgment.

3 Field Season

3.1 Observation conditions

Factors affecting observation conditions include wind velocity, seas, swell, cloud cover, glare, and precipitation. Wind strong enough to form whitecaps creates unacceptable observation conditions. Occasionally, when there is a short fetch, the water may be calm, but the wind is too strong to allow the pilot to fly concentric circles. Swell is only a problem when it is coupled with choppy seas. Cloud cover is desirable because it inhibits extreme sun-glade. Glare is a problem that can usually be moderated by observing from the side of the aircraft opposite the sun. Precipitation is usually not a problem unless it is extremely heavy.

Chop (C) and glare (G) are probably the most common and important factors effecting observation conditions. Chop is defined as any deviation from flat calm water up to whitecaps. Glare is defined as any amount of reflected light which may interfere with sight ability. After each transect is surveyed, presence is noted as C, G, or C/G and modified by a quartile (e.g. if 25% of the transect had chop and 100% had glare, observation conditions would be recorded as 1C/4G). Nothing is recorded in the conditions category if seas are calm and with no glare.

Observer fatigue

To ensure survey integrity, landing the plane and taking a break after approximately every 2 hours of survey time is essential for both observer and pilot. Survey quality will be compromised unless both are given a chance to exercise their legs, eat, relieve themselves, and give their eyes a break so they can remain alert.

Vessel activity

Areas with fishing or recreational vessel activity should still be surveyed.

Unique habitat features

Local knowledge of unique habitat features may warrant modification of survey protocol:

Extensive shoaling or shallow water (i.e. mudflats) may present the opportunity for extremely high sea otter densities with groups much too large to count with the same precision attainable in other survey areas. Photograph only otters within the strip or conduct complete counts, typically made in groups of five or ten otters at a time. Remember, groups >20 cannot initiate an ISU.

> Example: Orca Inlet, PWS. Bring a camera, a good lens, and extra memory cards. Timing is important when surveying Orca Inlet; the survey period should center around a positive high tide - plan on a morning high tide due to the high probability of afternoon winds and heavy glare. Survey the entire area from Hawkin's cutoff to Nelson Bay on the same high tide because sea otter distribution can shift dramatically with tidal ebb and flow in this region.

> **Cliffs** - How transects near cliffs are flown depends on the pilot's capabilities and prevailing weather conditions. For transects which intersect with cliff areas, including tidewater glaciers, discuss the following options with the pilot prior to surveying.

In some circumstances, simply increasing airspeed for turning power near cliffs may be acceptable. However, in steep/cliff-walled narrow passages and inlets, it may be deemed too dangerous to fly perpendicular to the shoreline. In this case, as with large groups of sea otters, obtain complete counts of the area when possible. In larger steep-walled bays, where it is too difficult or costly to obtain a complete count, first survey the entire bay shoreline 400 m out. Then survey the offshore transect sections, using the 400 m shoreline strip just surveyed as an approach. Because this is a survey design modification, these data will be analyzed separately.

Example: Herring Bay, PWS. Several cliff areas border this area.

Example: Barry Glacier, PWS. Winds coming off this and other tidewater glaciers may create a downdraft across the face. The pilot should be aware of such unsafe flying conditions and abort a transect if necessary.

Seabird colonies - Transects which intersect with seabird colonies should be shortened accordingly. These areas can be buffered for a certain distance dependant on factors such as colony size, species composition, and breeding status.

Example: Kodiak Island. Colonies located within 500m of a transect and Black-legged Kittiwakes > 100 OR total murres > 100 OR total birds > 1,000 were selected from the seabird colony catalog as being important to avoid.

Drifters - During calm seas, for whatever reason - possibly a combination of ocean current patterns and geography - large numbers of sea otters can be found resting relatively far offshore, over extremely deep water, miles (up to 4 miles is not uncommon) from the nearest possible foraging area.

Example: Port Wells, PWS. Hundreds of sea otters were found scattered throughout this area with flat calm seas on 2 consecutive survey years. As a result, Port Wells was reclassified and as high density stratum.

Glacial moraine - Similar to the drifter situation, sea otters may be found over deep water on either side of this glacial feature.

Example: Unakwik, PWS. Like Port Wells, Upper Unakwik was reclassified as high density stratum.

3.2 General methods

Prior to each survey, the following tasks are to be performed.

o Review the master field schedule (see SWAN protocol table 7) and prepare a list of tasks to be performed and set the field schedule
o Review personnel requirements, train personnel as needed, and make personnel assignments
o Arrange for aircraft charters as needed
o Prepare an itinerary and emergency contact list
o Assemble and distribute personal emergency and safety equipment

- o Arrange for travel of personnel to the flight origin site
- o Prepare plane for survey use, including operational and safety equipment (pilot's responsibility)
- o Review sampling procedures
  -Gather equipment and supplies including
  -Laptop computer with survey maps and waypoints, file transfer protocol to move waypoints to aircraft GPS (memory cards for Trimble GPS), data entry forms, databases, standard operating procedures, and other required software for data entry
  -Digital camera and accessories (memory sticks, cables for downloading images to a computer)
  -Aircraft GPS with waypoints loaded
  -Printed copies of transect maps at a resolution adequate to aid in navigation between endpoints (Figure 2)
  -High resolution binoculars (10 x 42 Leica recommended), 1 pair
  -Data sheets (forms 1and 2)
  -Batteries and battery chargers for electronics
  -Pencils, clipboards, permanent markers, and misc. office supplies
- o Ensure that electronics have fresh batteries and are in good working order

Preflight

Survey equipment: stopwatches (2)
binoculars (high resolution, compact)
clipboards (2)
transect maps
transect data forms (see below)
ISU data forms (see below)
list of transects waypoints
Global Positioning System (GPS)
memory cards with waypoints or other means of transferring transect waypoints to aircraft GPS
35 mm camera with 70-210 zoom lens
high-speed film (unless camera is digital)

Airplane windows must be cleaned each day prior to surveying.

Global Positioning System (GPS) coordinates used to locate transect starting and end points, must be entered as waypoints by hand or downloaded from an external source via a memory card.

Electrical tape markings on wing struts indicate the viewing angle and 400 m strip width when the aircraft wings are level at 300 feet (91.5 m) and the inside boundary is in-line with the outside edge of the airplane floats. These marks should be calibrated and adjusted as necessary for individual observers.

The following information is recorded at the top of each transect data and ISU form: (see appendix A for form 1: Aerial Survey Strip Transect Form and form 2: Sea Otter Aerial Survey ISU Data Form)

Date - Recorded in the mm/dd/yyyy format.
Observer – First and last names of observers
Pilot- Fist initial and complete last name of pilot
Aircraft - Should always be a Bellanca 180hp Scout on floats.
Area – Region and block (**if intensive block is only being sampled**).
Time begin - Military time.

3.3 Field Season Preparation – Planning an aerial survey

The sampling design described above requires delineating high and low density strata, establishing uniquely numbered systematic transects with discrete endpoints for each transect. Transect endpoints are points in space that the pilot must fly between, and the observer samples along, and must be transferred from the GIS software (ARC) where the transects are created to the GPS in the aircraft. The survey sampling design for the western Prince William Sound and the Alaska Peninsula intensive region (KATM) is illustrated in figures 5 and 6. The survey strata boundaries and transect endpoints will be established prior to survey implementation for each of the other intensive blocks (KEFJ). The aerial surveys will be designed prior to implementation of SWAN nearshore monitoring sea otter aerial survey, and will be derived from existing sampling designs previously sampled in each of the SWAN parks. These should not change appreciably between surveys, but revisions will likely require printing new maps and producing new waypoints for transects. The production of new survey designs and creation of transect waypoints and shoreline maps require advanced GIS skills. The necessary ARC programs are available from the USGS Alaska Science Center, and the USFWS, Marine Mammals Management Office, Anchorage, AK. The analytical programs necessary to analyze the transect and ISU data and generate population estimates are available from those same offices, using SAS software.

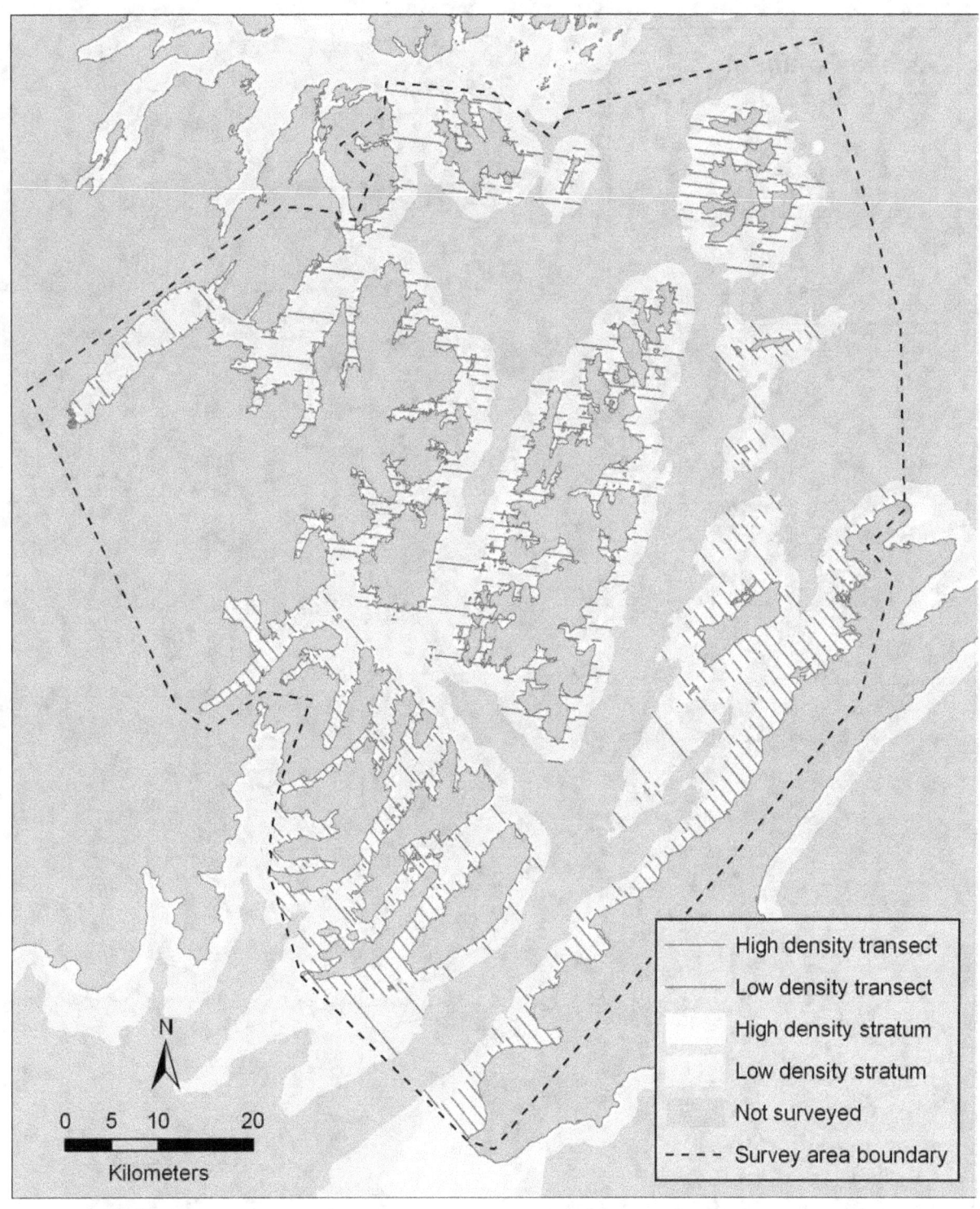

Figure 5. Survey Sampling Design Western Prince William Sound Region (Intensive block 8)

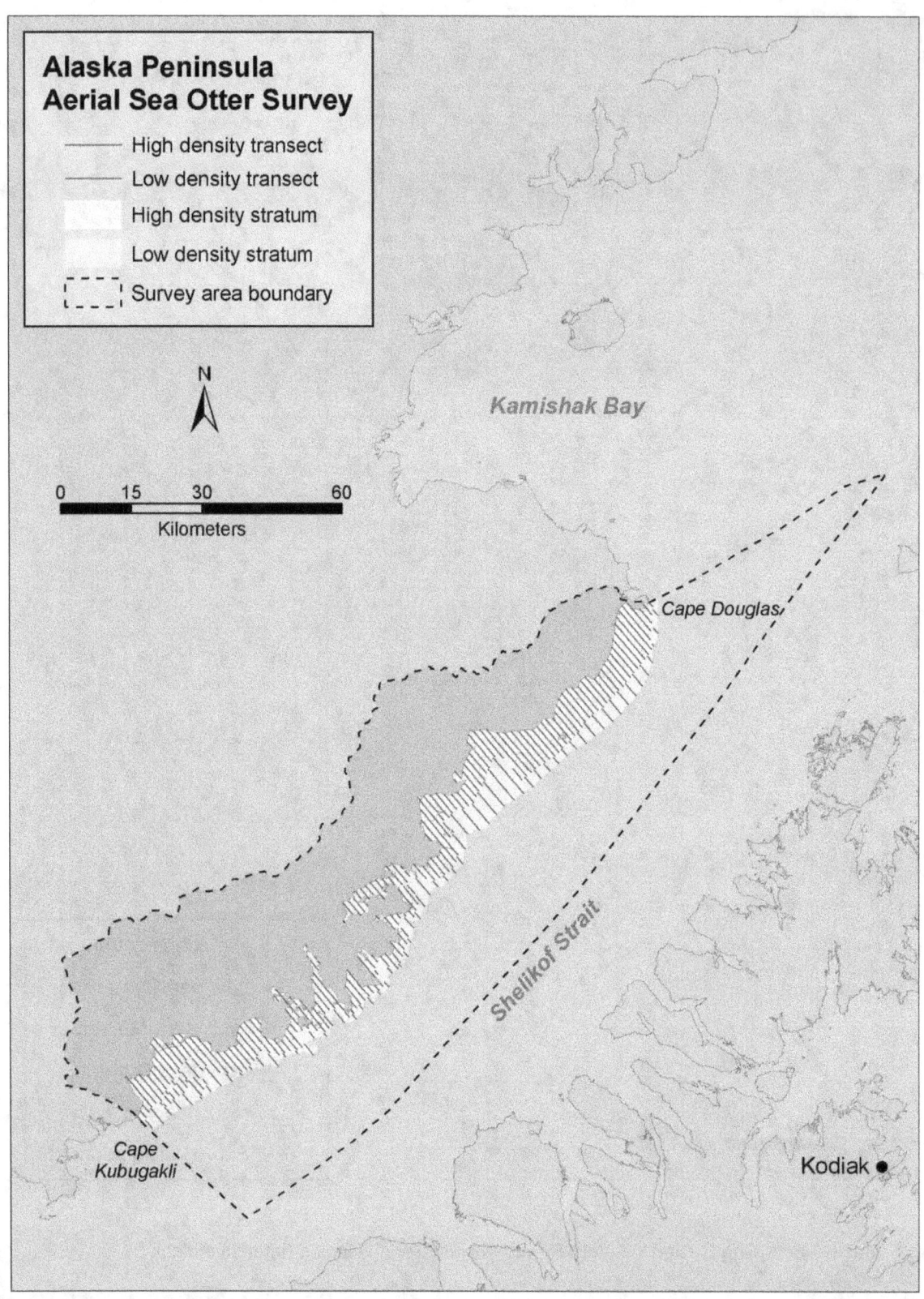

Figure 6. Survey Sampling Design Alaska Peninsula Region (Intensive block 10)

Several key points should be considered when planning an aerial survey:

1. Unless current sea otter distribution is already well known, it is well worth the effort to do some reconnaissance. This will help define the survey area and determine the number of observers needed, spacing of ISU's, etc.

2. Plan on using 1 observer per 5,000 otters.

3. Having an experienced technical pilot is extremely important. Low level flying is, by nature, a hazardous proposition with little room for error; many biologists are killed this way.

While safety is the foremost consideration, a pilot must also be skilled at highly technical flying. Survey methodology not only involves low-level flying, but also requires intimate familiarity with a GPS and the ability to fly in a straight line at a fixed heading with a fixed altitude, fixed speed, level wings, from and to fixed points in the sky. Consider the added challenge of flying concentric 400 meter circles, spotting other air traffic, managing fuel, dealing with wind and glare, traveling around fog banks, listening to radio traffic, looking at a survey map, and other distractions as well. Choose the best pilot available.

3.4 Sequence of Events
Prior to survey- Arrangements for dedicated and required aircraft support should be made several months in advance of the surveys work. Maps, electronic waypoint files, data recording and entry equipment, and data entry forms should be gathered and files tested for compatibility with GPS equipment in the aircraft.

Post survey- Review the transect data and survey design for completeness and the need for survey design revision. The most common need for survey revision includes revising the strata boundaries. This will usually be done when high densities of sea otters occur on low density transects (typically in proximity to high density strata). In consultation with others familiar with the survey design is acceptable to revise low density habitat to high density and the appropriate sampling intensity. Another common need for design revision includes joining short high density transects (usually slightly > 400 m) separated by short lengths (< 400 m) of low density strata. These revisions should be accomplished only following consultation with others familiar with this survey method.

Digitizing of all sea otters observed and all ISU's locations should take place shortly after completion of the survey. Data locations should be taken from the original data entry maps and digitized onto the actual GIS shoreline, bathymetry, and transect electronic files.

3.5 Recording Data
Prior to beginning the survey the observer and pilot should review this SOP. The survey should be conducted during the same 30 day period as in prior surveys of similar design and only under conditions described in this SOP. Sea otter number and location data are recorded directly on transect data sheets (See form 1) and on transect maps (see Figure 2) at the time of data collection. ISU data are recorded on ISU data entry forms (see form 2) and on transect maps (see Figure 2) at the time of data collection. The order of transect completion may vary over time,

largely dependent on logistics and weather conditions but all transects should be completed for each survey. Transects that are not surveyed are deleted from the sample during analysis, reducing the area sampled, but not the sample area. On a daily basis, following survey work, that days survey data should be reviewed for completeness and accuracy. Data entry should take place within 24 hours of collection, preferable the same day. Data should be backed up on a daily basis and stored away from the original data.

3.6 Post-collection Processing of Data
After each field day, the following tasks are to be completed:

- Field personnel are to review data sheets and edit as necessary to improve legibility and resolve any discrepancies.
- Enter data from data sheets into computer files. Verify the data entry.
- Download files from computers and digital cameras. Store these and provide additional documentation as needed.
- Make a backup copy (cd or other removable media) of all data collected.
- Check and replace batteries in electronic equipment as needed.
- Provide a summary of activities and observations for the day including any problems, suggestions for modifications in procedures, and unusual occurrences or observations.
- Prepare field sheets and equipment for the following day's use.

After each field trip or cruise, the following are to be completed:

- Produce a summary of the cruise based on summaries of daily activities and observations

3.7 End-of-season Procedures
At the end of each field season all equipment should be cleaned, serviced, and batteries removed for storage. Optics, and other equipment and field gear should be assessed for repair or replacement needs.

After each field season, the following are to be done:

- Clean and check all optical and electronic equipment and field gear for needed repair and store appropriately.
- Make repairs or obtain replacements for damaged or lost equipment or supplies.
- Produce a summary of the survey based on summaries of daily activities and observations. This should be completed within one week of completion of the seasons.

4 Data Handling, Analysis and Reporting

4.1 Metadata Procedures
See SWAN Sampling Protocol section 4.0

4.2 Overview of Database Design
See SWAN Sampling Protocol section 4.0

4.3 Data Entry, Verification and Editing
See SWAN Sampling Protocol section 4.0

4.4 Routine Data Summaries and Statistical Analyses
The overall analytical approach is described in the SWAN protocol that relies on data collected from most sampling protocols. In preparation of providing data derived from these surveys annual summaries should be completed. See appendix B Bodkin and Udevitz 1999 for survey data analytical procedures. Results of survey analysis will provide an estimate of sea otter abundance with a variance estimate. Plots and regression analysis of abundance estimates within intensive block and regions over time will be used to evaluate change in abundance. Examples of summarized data tables and plots follow:

Table 2. Table of results of sea otter abundance surveys in western Prince William Sound between 1993 and 2004.

Date	Western PWS		
	Population size	Std. Error	Propor. SE
Aug-93	2,054	698	0.34
Aug-94	2,228	356	0.16
Jul-95	2,185	225	0.10
Jul-96	2,180	218	0.10
Jul-97	2,341	202	0.09
Jul-98	3,119	494	0.16
Jul-99	2,475	381	0.15
Jul-00	2,658	294	0.11
Jul-01	.	.	.
Jul-02	1,840	334	0.18
Jul-03	2,631	540	0.21
Jul-04	2,704	315	0.12

Table 3. Table of results of sea otter abundance surveys in Prince William Sound between 1994 and 2003.

Prince William Sound				
	PWS without Orca Inlet		PWS with Orca Inlet	
	Population size	Std. Error	Population size	Std. Error
Aug 1994	9,092	1,422	14,352	2,418
Jul 1999	8,355	1,086	13,234	2,625
Jul 02	8,317	1,176	12,385	1,508
Jul 03	9,284	1,579	11,989	2,144

Sea Otter Population Trend in Western Prince William Sound 1993-2004

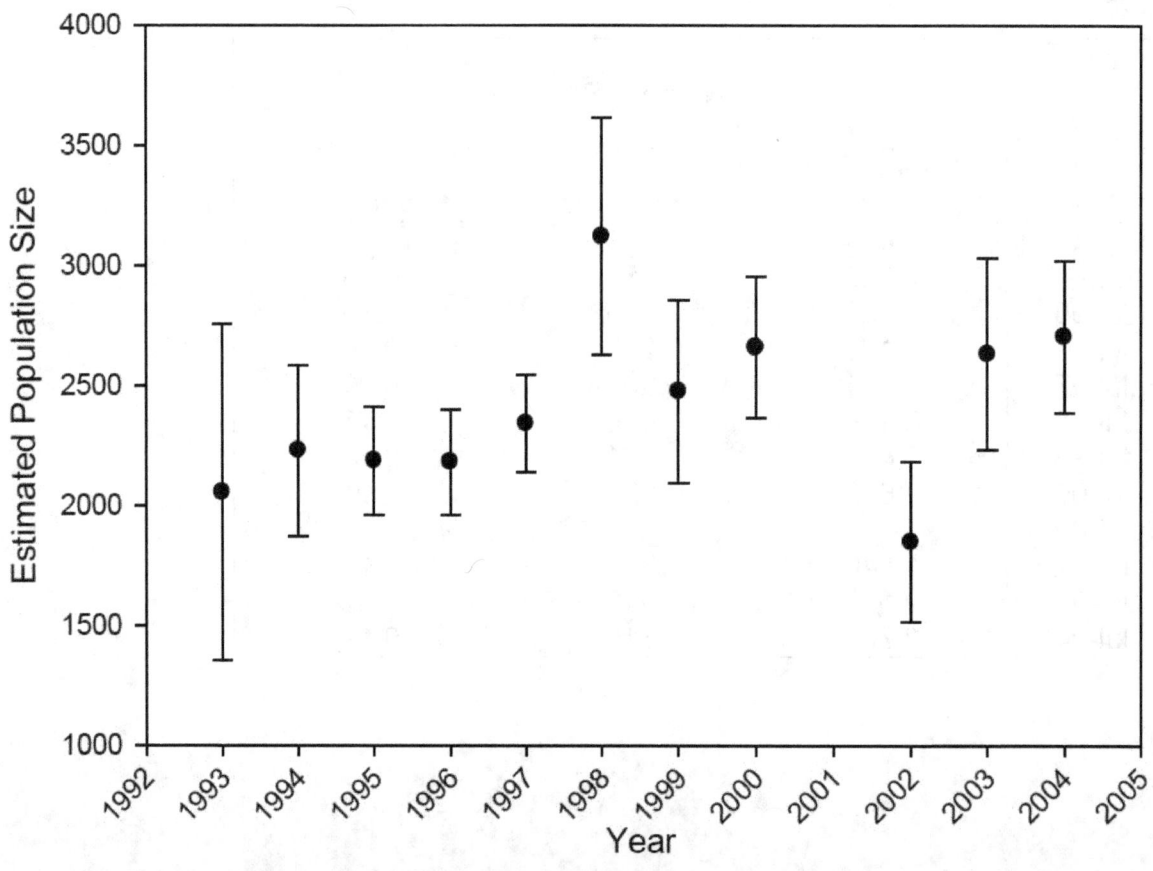

Figure 7. Plot of sea otter survey results in WPWS during 1993-2004.

4.5 Report Format

Reports will conform to specific guidelines set by the Natural Resource Publications Management website (http://www.nature.nps.gov/publications/NRPM/index.cfm). Reports will include maps, graphs, figures and other visuals to facilitate comprehension of findings.

4.6 Methods for Trend Analyses

Refer to the SWAN Protocol Narrative for Marine Nearshore Ecosystem Monitoring (Dean and Bodkin 2009 Draft).

4.7 Data Archival Procedures

Refer to the SWAN Protocol Narrative for Marine Nearshore Ecosystem Monitoring (Dean and Bodkin 2009 Draft).

4.8 Reporting

Refer to the SWAN Protocol Narrative for Marine Nearshore Ecosystem Monitoring (Dean and Bodkin 2009 Draft).

5 Personnel Requirements and Training

5.1 Roles and Responsibilities

Conducting the described aerial survey requires extensive training and testing. Each aerial observer must be tested against ground based observers (see Bodkin and Udevitz 1999, Appendix B) and achieve a sea otter detection probability from the air greater than 0.90 prior to conducting a survey. Training and testing will be conducted by personnel previously trained in the survey methodology and by observers experienced in shore based sea otter observation techniques. Pilots must be instructed by a pilot experienced in the survey methodology and tested by a trained and tested observer. All personnel must be current with applicable safety training including aircraft safety.

6 Operational Requirements and Workloads

6.1 Operational Requirements

Operational requirements include transportation and access to all SWAN regions for a two person crew consisting of a pilot and one aerial observer. Land based lodging, meals, fuel and a protected area to store plane overnight are required for each region surveyed. Depending on the area/region to be surveyed and weather conditions surveys can be conducted in 5-10 days. The two person crew must have access to survey maps, data forms, binoculars, electronics (e.g. stopwatches, digital camera, laptop computer and accessories, software and aircraft GPS). See section 3.2 for detailed list of supplies need. Pilot and observer must meet the personnel requirements and training stated above in section 5.0.

6.2 Annual Workload and Field Schedule

Workload 10 person days per year for field, 5 person days for lab analysis, per region. Logistics, housing, and meals at flight origination location. See master schedule for field schedule (See SWAN Protocol Table 7).

6.3 Start-up Costs and Budget Considerations

$2,000 for ARC software and $3,000 for aircraft GPS.

Annual costs include $11,000 annually for aircraft charter ($11,000 for NPS region) and $1,000 annually for per diem ($1,000 for NPS region).

7 Procedures for Revising the Protocol

All edits and amendments made to the protocol narrative and/or SOPs should be recorded in the revision history log table at the beginning of this document. Users of this protocol should promptly notify the project leader of the marine nearshore monitoring program of recommended edits or changes. The project leader will review and incorporate suggested changes as necessary, record these changes in the revision history log, and modify the date and version number on the title page of this document to reflect these changes.

8 Literature Cited

Bodkin, J. L. 2003. Sea Otter *Enhydra lutris*. *In* Wild Mammals of North America, 2nd edition. Feldhamer, G.A., B.C. Thompson, and J.A. Chapman. eds.. Wild Mammals of North America Biology, Management, and Conservation. John Hopkins University Press, Baltimore and London, pp 735-743.

Bodkin, J. L., B. E. Ballachey, T. A. Dean, A. K. Fukuyama, S. C. Jewett, L. McDonald, D. H. Monson, C. E. O'Clair, and G. R. VanBlaricom. 2002. Sea Otter Population Status and the Process of Recovery from the 1989 Exxon Valdez Oil Spill. Mar. Ecol. Prog. Ser. 241: 237-253.

Bodkin, J. L., and M. S. Udevitz. 1999. An aerial survey method to estimate sea otter abundanceG. W. Garner, S. C. Amstrup, J. L. Laake, B. F. J. Manly, L. L. McDonald, and D. G. Robertson. Marine Mammal Survey and Assessment Methods. A.A. Balkema, Rotterdam.

Cohen, J. 1998. J. Cohen. Statistical power analysis for the behavioral sciences. Lawerence Erlbaum Associates, Hillsdale, New Jersey.

Dean, T. A., J. L. Bodkin, A. K. Fukuyama, S. C. Jewett, D. H. Monson, C. E. O'Clair, and G. R. VanBlaricom. 2002. Sea Otter (*Enhydra lutris)* Perspective: Mechanisms of Impact and Potential Recovery of Nearshore Vertebrate Predators following the 1989 Exxon Valdez Oil Spill: Part B. Food Limitation and the Recovery of Sea Otters in Prince William Sound. Mar. Ecol. Prog. Ser. 241: 255-270.

Estes, J. A., and J. L. Bodkin. 2002. Otters. *In* Encyclopedia of Marine Mammals B. W. J. G. M. T. William F. Perrin, editors Academic Press

Estes, J. A., and D. O. Duggins. 1995. Sea Otters and Kelp Forests in Alaska: Generality and Variation in a Community Ecological Paradigm. Ecological Monographs. 65. (1.): 75-100.

Estes, J. A. and J. F. Palmisano. 1974. Sea Otters: Their Role in Structuring Nearshore Communities. Science. 185: 1058-1060.

Kenyon, K. W. 1969. N. American Fauna 68: The Sea Otter in the Eastern Pacific Ocean.

Monson, D. H., D. F. Doak, B. E. Ballachey, A. Johnson and J. L. Bodkin. 2000. Long-term impacts of the Exxon Valdez oil spill on sea otters, assessed through age-dependent mortality patterns. Proc. Natl. Acad. Sci. USA 97(12): 6562-6567.

Power, M.E., D. Tilman, J.A. Estes, B.A. Menge, W.J. Bond, L.S. Mills, G. Daily, J.C. Castilla, J. Lubchenco, and R.T. Paine. 1996. Challenges in the quest for keystones. BioScience 46:609-620.

Riedman, M. L. and J. A. Estes. 1990. The Sea Otter (Enhydra lutris): Behavior, Ecology, and Natural History. US Fish and Wildlife, National Technical Service. 90 (14).

Simenstad, C. A., J. A. Estes, and K. W. Kenyon. 1978. Aleuts, Sea Otters, and Alternative Stable-State Communities. Science. 200: 403-411.

Udevitz, M. S., J. L. Bodkin, and D. P. Costa. 1995. Detection of Sea Otters in Boat-Based Surveys of Prince William Sound, Alaska. Marine Mammal Science. 11. (1.): 59-71.

9 Appendices

9.1 Appendix A: Data Forms and Data Dictionaries

Form 1: Sea Otter Aerial Survey Strip Transect Form

Date:	Observer:	Start time:
Aircraft:	Pilot:	Area:

Transect number	Strip count (Adults/Pups)	Chop (1-4)	Glare (1-4)	ISU no.	Small group total	Complete count total
				Page totals =		

Data dictionary for data fields in Form 1, Sea Otter Aerial Survey Strip Transect Form.

Header data

Date: Day month year (dd/month/yyyy), with day and year in numerals and month in letters (e.g. 14 June 2007)

Observers: First and last names of observers (e.g. **Bill Smith**).

Start time of collection: Use the 24 hour clock (e.g. **0745**).

Aircraft: Should always be a Bellance 180hp Scout on floats. Enter Scout on strip form.

Pilot: Enter pilots first initial and last name of pilot (e.g. P Kearney)

Area: The N-REM region and block (**enter block number if intensive block is only being sampled**) in which the data were collected: **PWS** (Prince William Sound), **KP** (Kenai Peninsula), **KOD** (Kodiak archipelago), or **AP** (Alaska Peninsula). **Also enter map set number.**

Intensive site #: The number **(1-5)** of the intensive intertidal invertebrate and algal sampling site associated with this data collection.

Coordinates (Latitude/Longitude in decimal degrees, WG 84): The latitude and longitude in projection WG-84, at the nest site #.

Body of data form:

Transect number: Enter the transect number being flown at the time (e.g. 148) up to three digits

Strip count (adults/pups): Enter number of otters on strip count. **If no otters are detected enter a "0".** If an adult without a pup is detected enter number present (e.g. 1, 3 ect.). If there are adults with pups enter as adult(s)/pup(s) (e.g. 1/1 =one adult/one pup or 7/3 = seven adults and three pup. Enter marine mammals including harbor porpoise, seals and whales seen along the transect.

Chop (1-4): Chop (C) is defined as any deviation from flat calm water up to whitecaps. Chop (C) and glare (G) are probably the most common and important factors effecting observation conditions. **Nothing is recorded in the conditions category if seas are calm and with no glare.** After each transect is surveyed, presence is noted as C, G, or C/G and modified by a quartile (e.g. if 25% of the transect had chop and 100% had glare, observation conditions would be recorded as 1C/4G).

Glare (1-4): Glare (G) is defined as any amount of reflected light which may interfere with sight ability. Chop (C) and glare (G) are probably the most common and important factors effecting observation conditions. **If there is 50% or greater glare the ISU should be aborted.**

ISU no.: Is the sequential number of an intensive search unit (ISU). The first ISU initiated by the observer when flying a transect will be entered as 1. Out of 32 transects you could have zero ISUs, 6 or more it depends on the number of otters and the observer as to when an ISU is initiated.

Group of otters: A group of otters is defined as one or more otters separated by less than 4 meters. A comma between a number signifies a separate group (e.g. 2, 1, 1, 1 = 4 groups of otters with a total of 5 adults and zero pups).

Small group total: A group of otters is defined as one or more otters separated by less than 4 meters. A comma between each number signifies a group. There may be larger groups that you will count and enter on the strip count. You could have 1, 2 (or more) groups of otters on a strip count. If your strip count had 2 groups and is entered as 2, 7/3 than you enter 9/3 (9/3 = 9 adults/3 pups) in the small group total. You combine your groups and put all adults together and all pups together.

Complete count total: Complete count (cc) is for larger groups of otters seen on a transect. Circle the group and write "cc". For example on transect 213 you enter 5 groups of otters total. 2,1,1,1 (equals 4 groups) and 42/13 cc is another large group on the strip count. Your small group total will be 5 adult otters entered as 5/0 and the complete count (cc) total will be for the large group of 42 adults and 13 pups and is entered as 42/13 cc.. **If a complete count is done there should not be an ISU number associated with that transect.**

Page totals =: Add up and enter separately the totals from each page for both small group and complete group columns. For example; small group total = 37/1 and complete count total = 42/13

Notes: Be sure to write the page number at top right hand corner along with the date. Example: Pg. 2 entered 5/5/03

Form 2: Sea Otter Aerial Survey ISU Data Form

Date: Start Time:	Region:	Observer: Block:

Transect #:		ISU #:
Group #	Strip Count	Circle Count
1		
2		
3		
4		
5		

Transect #:		ISU #:
Group #	Strip Count	Circle Count
1		
2		
3		
4		
5		

Transect #:		ISU #:
Group #	Strip Count	Circle Count
1		
2		
3		

4		
5		

Data dictionary for data fields in Form 2:- Sea Otter Aerial Survey ISU form

Header data

Date: Day month year (dd/month/yyyy), with day and year in numerals and month in letters (e.g. 14 June 2007)

Observers: First and last names of observers (e.g. **Bill Smith**).

Start time of collection: Use the 24 hour clock (e.g. **0745**).

Aircraft: Should always be a Bellance 180hp Scout on floats. Enter Scout on strip form.

Pilot: Enter pilots first initial and last name of pilot (e.g. P Kearney)

Area: The N-REM region and block (**enter block number if intensive block is only being sampled**) in which the data were collected: **PWS** (Prince William Sound), **KP** (Kenai Peninsula), **KOD** (Kodiak archipelago), or **AP** (Alaska Peninsula). **Also enter map set number.**

Intensive site #: The number (**1-5**) of the intensive intertidal invertebrate and algal sampling site associated with this data collection.

Body of data form:

Circles: Draw landmarks (e.g. shoreline, large rocks and or mountains and cliffs) and mark otter numbers and activity within the ISU. Also enter 4 letter abbreviations of any marine mammals sighted in ISU. **Codes for otter activity are: Non-diving (N) or Diving (D).**

Transect #: Enter the transect number being flown at the time (e.g. 148) up to three digits

ISU #: Is the sequential number of an intensive search unit (ISU). The first ISU initiated by the observer when flying a transect will be entered as 1. Out of 32 transects you could have zero ISUs, 6 or more it depends on the number of otters and the observer as to when an ISU is initiated.

Group #: A group of otters is defined as one or more otters separated by less than 4 meters. A comma between a number signifies a separate group (e.g. 2, 1, 1, 1 = 4 groups of otters with a total of 5 adults and zero pups).

Strip count: Write the number of otters observed in each group along with their behavior. There are only two types of behavior recorded: Non-diving (N) or Diving (D). For example Transect # 438, ISU # 1, group # 1, Strip count 1/1d (one adult/one pup diving)

Notes: Be sure to write the page number at top right hand corner along with the date. Example: Pg. 2 entered 5/5/03

Circle Count:
Special rules regarding ISU's

1. **Mistaken identity** – When an ISU is mistakenly initiated by anything other than a sea otter (e.g. bird, rock, or floating debris), the flight path should continue for one full circle until back on transect. At this point the ISU is to be abandoned as if it was never initiated and the normal flight path is resumed.

2. **Otters sighted outside an ISU** – Otters sighted outside an ISU which are noticed during ISU cir les are counted only when the ISU is completed, normal flight path has been resumed, and they are observed on the strip.

9.2 Appendix B: Required Reading

Bodkin and
Udevitz_1999

Dean et al. 2002

NPS 953/107692, May 2011